MEMORY

Make It Better to Make Life Better

Everyone has one

Everyone wants a *good* one

Yes! **Everyone** can have a good one, at any age

D.R. Martin, PhD*
(*Personal human Development)

SmartyPants Press
Falmouth, Maine 04105
www.SmartyPantsSecrets.com

ISBN 13: 978-1-943971-04-6
ISBN 10: 1943971048

The SmartyPants Secrets Concept

A **SmartyPants Secret** is that **one piece of information** that you need to know to make every job a little bit, or maybe a lot, **easier**. Almost everything we do in life has a SmartyPants secret that to it, that knowing the "secret" would help tremendously in shortening the learning curve.

After experiencing many "a ha!" moments that were previous head bangers, I realized that there was a lot of grief – i.e. aggravation, wasted time, spent resources - that could have been saved if I had known to tap into the insider information that others had and I was lacking. A SmartyPants secret is that crucial bit of timely knowledge.

We all want a magic bullet answer that solves all of our problems in one fell swoop and makes everything go perfectly well, preferably in record time! We want that magic to happen right NOW, to be easily done, and to be preferably cheap, or at least not at great expense. There are a lot of demands on our unattainable magic ☺

For example, one day I looked at my face and damn if I didn't see a "sun spot" (nastily also called a "liver" spot) marring the surface of my otherwise smooth face on the right lower cheek. I scheduled an appointment at the dermatologist to verify the find and see if it could be lasered off. She sent me to an aesthetician who gave me some key information that made a huge difference in my decision of what to do next.

I was told that my even slightly darker (Asian) skin carries more pigment than Caucasian skin obviously. But what's not obvious is the way the body works, specifically the way the skin works, which is that when you wound the skin's surface, which laser surgery would certainly do, extra pigments rush to the spot to heal it (the "job" of pigment is to protect the underlying cells). The net result is that non-Caucasian skin heals into darker scabs and scars. (I have noticed this phenomena before but never made a direct connection.) Why then would I ever choose to have laser surgery on my face to remove a mark only to end up with an even darker mark? Yikes!

Obviously I wouldn't, but without this specialized knowledge about different results with different skin types, that even the dermatologist didn't know (yes, she was the recommender of the laser surgery option) I would've made a poor decision, with permanent negative results. A SmartyPants timely secret to the rescue!

Experts, who have hours of experience doing what the newbie is attempting to do, have expert knowledge, which may not be so secret, but it is **key information** that the novice greatly needs.

If you've ever struggled with something then learned the 'something' afterwards that caused you to say to yourself or to say aloud, "*Well, **if I only known THAT before I did this**, it would've made a world of difference!*" then you just learned a SmartyPants secret - the hard way.

The short SmartyPants Secrets books give you the secret that you need on a given topic, the most important piece of information that makes the greatest difference between easier success and hard-fought failure.

When I was young there was a professor at Cornell University, which in his obituary listed him as "***the last man to know everything***." I was taken by the concept of anyone knowing everything there is to know contained in one brain. Oh, to have such a mind!

But **to know everything**, logical facts and figures, and **to be able to do everything** are **two different things**. Brain power doesn't equal skill and expertise.

Today that one brain that knows everything is the Internet. There is so much information today available on the Internet; we can all be like that professor at Cornell and have access to all knowledge at the click of our fingertips.

More knowledge than we could ever consume - **who has time** to go through it all? Most of the time **what you really want is to know is the crux of the subject** on hand, not the whole litany of everything imaginable that is available to know.

Tell me just what I need to know! (and I likely don't know what specific knowledge to ask for). It's literally impossible to know what you don't know. Let the expertise of knowledgeable others guide you.

If you are new to a topic the **SmartyPants secret can save you time and effort**, which are important to your success. Not a complete course on the topic, which you can certainly get elsewhere, the SmartyPants secrets concept is primarily to help you **not miss the key information needed for success**.

The building block of knowledge that the foundation rests upon; the Keystone or cornerstone knowledge makes a critical difference, especially when that knowledge that you do have, or think you have, is **faulty, incomplete or missing** entirely.

The concept of **social proof** states that when we have no prior experience in a given situation we rely on **others to show us the way**. We believe that lacking personal knowledge, that their situation is similar to our situation, and therefore what worked for them has a high probability of working for us.

We quiz others about our shared circumstances around the situation to verify that their solution is a good one. Plus, we think: *there's nothing to lose in trying since I don't have a better answer*.

Then when what worked for another doesn't happen to work for us, we are reminded that **we are all different people**, with different variables that impact success or failure. Some solutions to problems are hit or miss depending on who we are. And sometimes success depends on having and following the right key knowledge.

Solving problems is not the complete SmartyPants concept, although SmartyPants secrets can indeed offer real help for real problems. Rather the full concept is that having that key knowledge piece makes efforts easier and successful quicker; hopefully **avoiding having the problem in the first place**. We do anything in life because we have a goal to achieve. Reaching that goal successfully, quickly and easier than without knowing the SmartPants secret is the SmartyPants concept.

And because **all SmartyPants secrets have a physiological root**, grounded in our shared human biology, every SmartyPants secret is valid for everyone, no matter who you are. While we are all uniquely different from each other, we have a **common biology** consisting of inherited traits that stretch back to the Neanderthal era.

Applying a SmartyPants secret **will work for you no matter who you are**. And in our busy world, who doesn't want to save time and know the SmartyPants secret to anything?

Why ever risk hindering easier success by not knowing the core success secret?

MEMORY

Retrieving Elusive Recall of Lists, Names, Items Tucked Away...and Where Did I Put Down My Cell Phone/Glasses/Car Keys...?

THE AGED AND THE NOT SO AGED

Ahh, we think memory issues are a 'privilege' for the aged, but not so. Perhaps admitting to having a 'senior moment' makes us feel better, pushing any memory issues to the realm of senior citizens. However this fallacy is dispelled by neuroscience, finding no decline in functional brain capacity as we age, putting aside disease impairment.

If you are not among the aged, but find that you have more memory lapses than you like, that the off moments are more common than not, well admitting that your brain isn't as sharp as it was is the real rub. But that can be changed. And if you are aged and are trying to regain some of your old memory sharpness, great – this is the right place to be for you too. A good memory is possible for anyone, at any age.

Studies have shown that the brain is very 'plastic', the term coined to reference the ability of the brain to rebuild itself with new neural connections to almost limitless capacity. But, you wonder, what about those thousands of neurons you hear are dying every day? Now that we're older, isn't it a bit too late? True, we do lose thousands of neurons daily, but the flip side of that knowledge coin is that we have billions and billions of neurons we never use – more neurons than all the stars in the galaxy – inside of each of our fabulous brains. We will never run out of neurons, not matter how old we get, how many die off, or how many we use.

The concept of only using 10% of our brains comes from this fact; we grossly under-utilize our brain power, wasting 90%. We all have the potential to be geniuses, if we would develop that gray matter between our ears just a tiny bit more!

Memory lives inside neural connections. The more of these vital connections that we can make to attach to each memory, the stronger the memory will be, and the easier the memory will be to retrieve.

GOOD NEWS AND BAD NEWS

So the good news is: we can increase our brain power at any age, and gain strong memories.

But the bad news is: it's work to build the brain 'muscle'. Just like a muscle, the brain must be built up, worked, exercised, and developed for strength. Just like a muscle, 'use it or lose it' applies to the brain.

And a second piece of bad news is: we cannot retrieve the past, we can only move forward. We can't go back and re-encode all our old memories for total recall of everything learned and experienced over years of living, but we can move forward with strong future memories. Old memories aren't gone forever, they are just hard to retrieve because we didn't lay down a good neural path to find them. But once you understand the concept and develop a process for the future, you have all those future memories coming to encode properly.

Are you willing to put in some work to get a better memory? It's not hard work, but it does require changing some mental habits. But then you knew, deep down you knew, that there would be some work involved. There is no magical trick to instantly having great recall, but there is a future path. If you choose to take it, you have nothing to lose and everything to gain.

While we could all say we've logged our fair share of time into trying to remember things, I'm going to put forth that I have expertise on this topic to be your guide because I have spent many many hours not only using my memory like all of you, but unlike you I have also spent hours researching and applying that knowledge into practice, which is likely different from your experience with memory.

My personal reading library contains well over 1000 books, with 450 volumes of reference books alone on a variety of nonfiction business related topics. Not only have I read more than half of these volumes from cover to cover, but I also retain much of the knowledge of what I read, to then be able to crossover different pieces of knowledge together and apply them in unique combinations. So you gain the benefit of my efforts, which saves you putting in the time yourself, *making you a true SmartyPants*, for knowing to take the shortest knowledge route ☺

Have you ever thought or said any of these things:

➢ *"Now where did I put my car keys / eyeglasses / cell phone? [again!]"*

➢ *"Did I remember to lock the door/turn off the stove?"*

➢ *"I JUST had that in my hand and now it's disappeared… (Did you happen to take it?)"*

➢ *"I must not forget to bring _____ with me when I leave the house"*

➢ *"I feel like I'm forgetting something important that I want to remember, but I just can't remember what it is…"*

➢ *"I need to run five errands/pick up five things at the store and don't have the list on me and can't remember all the items on the list"*

➢ *"I have great ideas when I go to bed at night, but in the morning I just can't remember any of them – but I KNOW that they were great ideas and worth remembering!"*

➢ *"I hid that important/valuable item in a really safe place so I wouldn't lose it, but now I can't remember where that 'safe place' is"*

➢ *"I can never remember the punch line of jokes to re-tell them"*

➢ *"What was his/your name again?"*

➢ *"The name is familiar but I can't remember what she looks like/put a face to the name"*

THE JOURNEY TO A STRONG MEMORY

We'll start first with a very **broad overview of the brain**, where memory comes from.

From there we'll discuss the **types of memory**, how memory is created, and basic **memory principles**.

Then on to **memory systems**, techniques that you can learn and use to improve your memory

Finally ending with the **Smarty-Pants Secret** that will make the difference, that one thing you really need to know to be successful in improving your memory.

MAJOR MEMORY PROBLEMS

Most people have memory issues around a few problematic areas:

☹ Absentmindedness

"Where did I put my car keys / eyeglasses / cell phone?"

"Did I remember to lock the door / turn off the stove?"

"I JUST had that in my hand and now it's disappeared... (Did you perhaps take it?)"

☹ Short-term memory retrieval

"I must not forget to bring _____ with me when I leave"

"I feel like I'm forgetting something important that I want to remember, but I just don't know what it is"

"I need to run five errands/pick up five things at the store and don't have the list on me and can't remember all the items on the list"

"I have great ideas when I go to bed at night, but in the morning I just can't remember any of them, but know that they were great ideas and worth remembering!"

☹ Retrieval of old data

"*I hid that important/valuable item in a safe place so I wouldn't lose it, but now I can't remember where that 'safe place' is*"

"*I can never remember the punch line of jokes to re-tell them*"

"*I can't remember a thing I learned in school*"

☹ Remembering names and faces

"*What was his/your name again?*"

"*The name is familiar but I can't remember what she looks like/put a face to the name*"

If any of these sound like you, then that's what this book will cover.

NOTE: This book will **not** be discussing specialized memory situations like - giving a speech (speaking without notes), taking a test knowledge retrieval (learning is a full subject for another Smarty-Pants Secrets book), reciting poetry, memorizing a deck of cards, and other parlor tricks. Those memory feats, which are not everyday concerns for most, are not within the scope of this book.

HAVING A GOOD MEMORY IS IMPORTANT

Mainly having a strong memory is important because when we forget something it makes us **feel bad about ourselves**, like we did **something wrong** that we are ashamed of; we **blame ourselves** because we think that somehow we should have remembered 'X'.

We even start to **feel old** and call the lapse a **'senior moment'** when in reality a poor memory has no correlation to aging. What does happen to our brains as we age is that our poor habits of not exercising our brains and developing good skills become ingrained and accepted as "part of the aging process" and these bad coping habits are hard to change.

Memory is built on practice, training in a system, and the plasticity of the brain, which has the ability to keep changing and improving right up until we die. Therefore **the older we get, rather than decline, the better our memory can become.**

Having a good memory gives you a **business edge, a social edge, and is a boost to self-esteem + confidence**, important at any age.

MEMORY BLOCKS

Any discussion on memory must briefly touch upon blocks that prevent knowledge retrieval. Memory blocks can be emotional, mechanical, or physical.

Emotional memory blocks usually result from past conflict which the brain puts into place for protection, a survival mechanism.

Mechanical memory blocks are due to an overload of information, resulting in poor or muddled connections as the brain fails to properly file or mis-encodes bits of information into long-term memory.

Physical memory blocks are due to illness, dementia, amnesia, or any time the body is not in optimal health, impaired in any way, due to alcohol, drugs, stress, poor diet, lack of exercise, etc. - which all can block memory

Emotional, mechanical, and physical memory blocks coverage in greater detail beyond this cursory description are also not within the scope of this book. If needed, support for any deep memory blocking issues should be sought elsewhere.

Starting at the top – A Brief Treatment of BRAIN BASICS

The brain consists of 3 layers:

- The reptilian brain, that controls our very basic functions, BRAIN STEM

- The limbic system, where emotions are centered, CEREBELLUM

- The neocortex, where higher thinking is developed, CEREBRUM

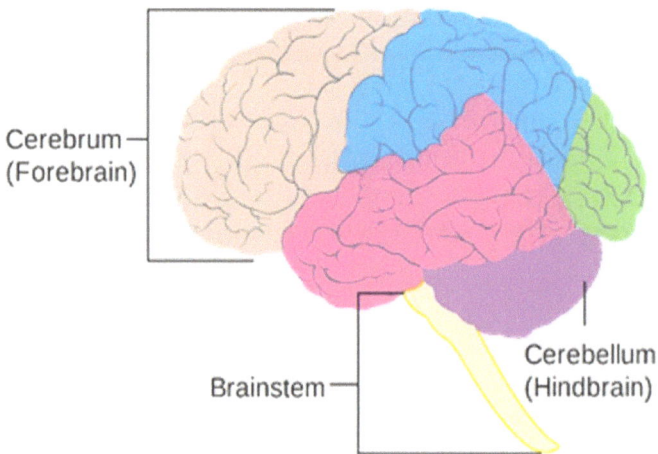

Cerebrum (Forebrain)

Brainstem

Cerebellum (Hindbrain)

Memory works best when hooked to other major cerebrum areas: the senses – SIGHT, HEARING, TOUCH, TASTE, SMELL+MOVEMENT.

Input arrives to the brain via the senses. Hooking the input to the other senses helps to make the memory sticky, by creating new neural pathways, which travel to the different senses. With multiple connections, retrieval of the memory happens more easily.

LEFT AND RIGHT BRAIN HEMISPHERES

The two brain sides are attributed with different traits:

LEFT brain: logic, words, lists, numbers, sequence, analysis

RIGHT brain: rhythm, imagination, intuition, daydreaming, color, dimension, spacial properties

Importantly: *WE NEED BOTH SIDES OF THE BRAIN WORKING TOGETHER TO CREATE THE MOST EFFECTIVE MEMORIES*

How memory works

sensory
input

long term
memory

meaningful
output

filter

short term
memory

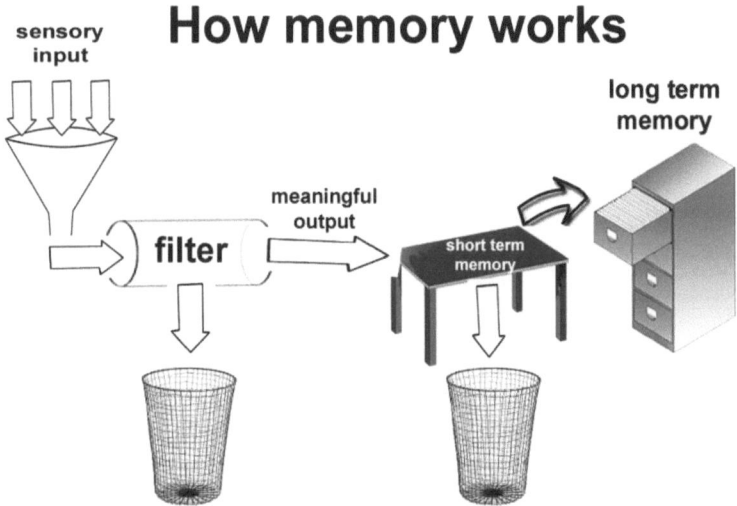

Data comes in to the brain funnel via the
senses. Some stuff gets filtered out (not
paying attention, dismissed as already known,
inaccurate assumptions) and some lands on
the short term memory table. But the table is
just a temporary (and small) holding place,
and what isn't lost to time – short term is
appropriately named – the important
memorable stuff is encoded into long term
memory, for later retrieval.

Except when there are coding problems, or
poor coding, then the retrieval of that memory
is iffy...

LONG TERM MEMORY CODING ISSUES

CODING PROBLEMS when sent to long term memory storage necessarily result in **RETRIEVAL PROBLEMS**

bird? bins? bans? band? bard? bars? bind?

firs? find? fins? fans?

Hmmm…What do you think?

How can poorly encoded, fuzzy, unclear memories be retrieved with any accuracy???

Conscious coding is the solution to memory retrieval issues – have a defined system to encode the memory for easy retrieval.

Developing the coding habit makes future memory strong.

10 Memory Principles

Memories must be coded, with a systematic process, to be retained. Here are the 10 avenues to use in creating strong encoded memories, for easiest retrieval; include not one but several elements!

- **Sensory** - employ as many senses as possible, not just sight, also sound, smell, taste, touch, texture

- **Association** – what's the associated thought connection of this image?

- **Humor** – make the mental image to be remembered do and say silly things!

- **Imagination** – how creative can you be? Wild and crazy = memorable

- **Number** – existing in long term already

- **Symbolism** – is there meaning?

- **Color** – bright, attention getting

- **Order/Sequence** – tells a story

- **Positive/Pleasant** – vs scary, negative

- **Exaggeration** – bigger is better

WAYS TO REMEMBER

✓ **Rote** –repeat, repeat, keep repeating. This is how we learned math tables, the state capitals – sometimes it sticks, with repeated ingraining (i.e. math) and sometimes it doesn't (what's the capital of Oregon?). We still use this short term to remember phone numbers, directions.

✓ **Association** – Create a picture of what you want to remember, incorporating several of the 10 memory principles above, to encode that memory into long term, but remember to create the picture *immediately*

✓ **Mind maps** – a visual memory layout system to remember a large body of knowledge, best used with studying for tests, speeches, presentations.

✓ **Link & peg system** - Link the wanted memory to a peg/hook in an established system, of which there are several systems to explore, up next.

✓ **Mnemonic devices** – using the first letter to spell a word or sentence

LINK & PEG SYSTEM: Memory Palace (the most popular one)

Your childhood home.

Most people like this memory system best because it's the easiest to use, since you have your childhood home, your 'palace' already locked into long term memory for ready use.

Recall the layout of any well-known home or building, establish a patterned path to always follow when travelling through, then lay the item (link) to be remembered on the location (peg), for recall of hundreds of items, in order.

Remember to include as many of the memory principles as you can for best retrieval of the items – make them talk, make them move, exaggerate them and make them creatively silly.

Lock in each item separately and deliberately, taking only a second or two to create each.

Here's a short example of using the Memory Palace system in action:

My childhood home pattern starts with the 1) the driveway, 2) the breezeway steps, 3) the entry landing, 4) the doorknob, opens onto the kitchen, which leads to moving along the room's perimeter: 5) the refrigerator, 6) the counter, 7) the sink, 8) the dishwater, 9) the stove, 10) cupboard… now I could go drawer by drawer, or I could include all the countertop appliances, or I could move into the next room… 100s of possible locations. Once you have the link pattern established, it's easy to now peg the items to the links – what items?

EXERCISE: Remember these random items, in order

- **Calculator**

- **Dress**

- **Book**

- **Key**

- **Flashlight**

- **Pin**

- **Leonardo da Vinci**

- **Sofa**

- **Table**

- **Cigar**

Let's apply my Memory Palace system to the

first few items on the list –

1) I imagine that my driveway is actually a giant [exaggeration] calculator. When I step on the keys to get to the house, I can hear the beep-beep-beep [sounds] and see the numbers changing on the display [movement]

2) Climbing the breezeway steps, I look down and see the middle step isn't brick, it's a flowery red dress. I catch myself from almost tripping on the flowing fabric [movement], only to stub my toe on all the buttons [humor]. One of the flowers squirts fluid on my foot when stepped on and up wafts a fragrant floral essence [smell], lovely!

3) Stepping on the entry landing, which is to step on the pages of an open book; the pages turning slowly in the gentle breeze [movement]. The print rises off the pages and the letters spelling b-o-o-k float in the air [imagination] doing a little song and dance routine. I hear the sweet song the book sings [sound] and dance along for a bit.

Your own created memories will be most powerful to you, but be sure to include multiple elements, which will make retrieval easy.

LINK PEG SYSTEMS: Number Rhyme (my personal favorite)

Following the old children's nursery rhyme, peg the item to be remembered to the rhyming one-to-ten link object.

1 - thumb

2 - shoe

3 - knee

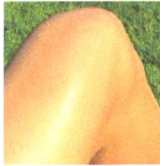

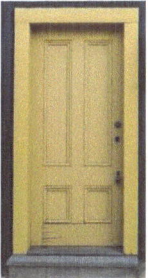

4 - door

5 - hive

6 - sticks

7 - heaven

8 - gate

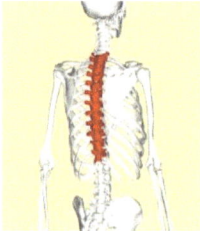

9 - spine

10 - hen

OK, that covers the first 10 items on the list, but how does the system account for remembering *item #11* and up? Easy - add **colors** to the pegs, following the pattern ROY G BIV – red, orange, yellow, green, blue, indigo, violet – *brights* to cover the first 70; then *pastels* for the next 70, as needed.

To see the rhyme link-peg memory system in action, let's re-number the list of recall items:

Item #1: **Calculator**

... Item #11: **Dress**

... Item #22 **Pin**

... Item #33 **Book**

1) I look at my **thumb, red** from pounding on the **calculator** keys embedded in the thumb's pad... (add more memory elements)

11) My **thumb, orange** from ink stamping a **dress** design on fabric, which will be made into an orange-faced doll's dress...

22) A large **pin** in my **shoe,** makes me pee all over it, turning the shoe **yellow.** The head of the pin is singing Yellow Submarine...

33) Kneeing on an open **book,** green ink leaks off the pages and onto my **knees,** turning them **green,** which makes the grass blades cheer out loud "yay!"...

And so on, encoding strong memories that are easily retrieved, when recall is needed.

LINK PEG SYSTEMS: Number shape (visual versus auditory)

If rhyming doesn't work for you, here's a link-peg system involving numeric shapes: determine a numeric order pegged to the visual shape of the numbers 1-10.

And you know how to handle 11-20, etc. – apply ROY G BIV color order here too.

Here's one shape-numeric link-peg system:

1. looks like a **paintbrush**

2. see the **swan**

3. (sideways) **heart**

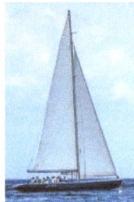

4. **sailboat** shows the number

5. **hook**

6. rolled **elephant trunk**

7. **cliff**

8. **hour glass**

9. **tadpole**

10. **bat and ball**

Putting the shape-numeric memory encoding link-peg system to use, here are some words:

> Item #1: **Calculator**
>
> ... Item #11: **Dress**
>
> ... Item #22 **Pin**
>
> **...** Item #33 **Book**

1) The **paintbrush** dripping with red paint, is painting **red** numbers on the **calculator**. The red display talks, saying "it all adds up"...

11) The slim fitting A-line **dress** looks like a giant **paintbrush**, the wooden handle is **orange** and the brush tip has been dipped in orange paint. She walks with a paint whoosh...

22) The beautiful **swan is yellow**, not white, bathed in golden sunlight. See that the beak is a large **pin** which the swan is deftly using to spear fish out of the water, squawking when it catches a fish with the sharp pin...

33) The **green heart** is a bookmark in the **book**, with the green standing for envy, a love story of betrayal – green juice squirts out of the heart with every page turned...

LINK PEG SYSTEMS: Alpha

With the Alpha system, the alphabet is the peg to link onto for 26 easy links, with the key of using peg images that carries *the initial sound* of the letter itself, not necessary beginning with the letter.

A. Ace

B. Bee

C. Sea

D. Deed

E. Easel

F. Effort

G. Jeans

H. H-bomb

I. Eye

J. Jay (bird)

K. Cake

L. Elevator, or elbow

M. Empty, or MC

N. Entire

O. Oboe

P. Pea

Q. Queue

R. Arch

S. Eskimo

T. Tea, or t-shirt

U. Ewe, or Yew

V. VIP, or VP

W. WC

X. X-ray

Y. Wife

Z. Zebra

So you now know the process to use this alpha link-peg system to encode memories for easy retrieval.

Just remember, whatever system you choose to use to 1) use as **many** memory principle elements as you can, which strengthens the memory with lots of connections, and 2) the **crazier** the back story, the better the recall!

REMEMBERING NAMES & FACES

Names are especially hard to remember because most **names have no object connection** to visually associate with.

Girls named after flowers (*Rose, Daisy*) or boys named after animals (*Wolf, Bear*) are easier, but still are not a given that you will remember (which flower name was it?)

Names are nothing more than a string of letters in combination with no basis for existence other than being a person's name - what is a '*Mary*' or a '*John*'? – which is why unique name creation is popular and easy to do for trendsetting parents, choosing not to follow the common name route.

Names require **straight rote** memorization to retain in long term memory. Foreign names can be especially problematic as the letter combinations are not always in known familiar language patterns.

With rote, you say their name over and over again, aloud in conversation (which I find rather annoying) or in your head (making it harder to focus on what they're actually saying) in the hopes that you will retain their name, moving it into your long term memory through continuous repetition. This method isn't helpful when you don't see the person frequently enough, then are at a loss for their name the next time you happen to see them.

Another name remembering technique is to think of another person you happen to know with the same name as this new person, then associate some trait that the two people may have in common. Great if you know someone with the same name (and they usually have nothing in common to latch on to...) but with all the different names around today, this option is hardly reliable.

Since our brains are heavily visual and rely mainly on sight for data input, the best way to remember names is to look at the person's face (which, unlike attire, doesn't change), looking for the outstanding feature (what's most striking?) and associating their name, a part of their name, a rhyme to their name with that facial feature, or with a trait associated with that facial feature. Not easy, I know, but that's the best system in use, in a hard process.

Let's give it a try, to see this name remembering technique in action.

Meet: **Karen DiMarco**   Meet: **Bill Ashton**

KAREN – her most striking feature are her piercing eyes; she must really 'care' about what she's looking at so intently, so I'll think care → Karen when I look at those eyes.

DiMARCO – it's like she's 'marking' out her prey, 'de-marking' the target.

BILL – you notice those heavy glasses right away, and think "those must have cost a hefty 'bill' ".

ASHTON – those small eyes are full of 'ash', and those glasses weigh a 'ton'.

So remembering names and faces isn't easy, but is definitely doable, IF you take the time with the process upon meeting, AND you allow your imagination free reign.

MNEMONICS

Remember how you remembered the names of the planets in grade school? "*My Very Educated Mother Just Showed Us Nine Planets*". Ignoring the fact that Pluto's planetary status is currently called into question, this mnemonic device was a great way to remember the planets, in the right order from the sun.

HOMES is another word mnemonic to remember the Great Lakes.

And the notes that pertained to the lines on a music scale – sentence mnemonic again to the rescue! – *Every Good Boy Deserves Fudge* (with **FACE** for notes names of the spaces).

So using mnemonics is a handy device, but is best when coupled with **rote** (as in above examples), with **written**, or with a **visual trigger.** Otherwise how do you remember the word or the sentence of the mnemonics in the first place?

As a memory device, that trigger can be a physical object or a strong visual image that tells the story of the mnemonic sentence; recall that to trigger a good memory, create a crazy story including many sensory elements.

USING SPECIFIC MEMORY HELPS IN CONTEXT

Let's go back to our initial questions and address some common memory issues, to review the best system solution for each:

"Now where did I put my car keys / eyeglasses / cell phone? [yet again!]"
→ Use **ASSOCIATION** <u>immediately</u> when the item leaves your hands to encode the item to the mundane location, using multiple elements to remind you – car keys on the counter? A large talking hand emerges from the counter and says, "I have an iron grip on these keys!"

"Did I remember to lock the door/turn off the stove?"
→ Use **ASSOCIATION** <u>immediately</u> after doing the action to remind yourself that you indeed did it, using <u>multiple</u> elements (sound, visual, exaggeration, imagination) in your memory – the stove speaks up and says, "Yep, all turned off" or a hand emerges from the doorknob to pat you on the back with a "Thanks for locking me up tight."

"I JUST had that in my hand and now it's disappeared... *(Did you take it?)***"**
→ Immediacy of memory creation is the keystone habit to develop. Use **ASSOCIATION** immediately <u>as the item</u>

leaves your hands to encode the item to the unplanned location, using multiple elements to connect back to. (And don't blame others for your memory lapses.)

"I must not forget to bring _____ with me when I leave the house"
→ Give yourself a visual **MEMORY AID** – a can't miss note, a giant version of the item itself blocking your exit, a related reminder item in a spot that must be looked at on the way out – to help trigger the wanted memory.

"I feel like I'm forgetting something important that I want to remember, but I just don't know what it is..."
→ Use an established **LINK-PEG system** to create a To Do list in the first place.

"I need to run five errands/pick up five things at the store and don't have the list on me and can't remember all the items on the list"
→ Use an established **LINK-PEG system** to create the shopping/errands list initially before heading out.

"I have great ideas when I go to bed at night, but in the morning I just can't remember any of them - just that they were great and worth remembering!"
→ While lying in bed before falling asleep, hook the great idea to your regularly used

40

LINK-PEG system for idea retrieval in the morning, or it will be lost with no hook!

"I hid that important/valuable item in a really safe place so I wouldn't lose it, but now I can't remember where that 'safe place' is"
→ Use **ASSOCIATION** <u>immediately</u> to encode the hidden item's location to the item, associating the item with the unique location; anytime the item is thought about, the memory of the location, with all the elements encoded, will come to mind.

"I can never remember the punch line of jokes to re-tell them"
→ Put the joke in story format, use ROTE repeatedly on the punchline to get it exactly right, then tell the story with the ending well memorized through repetition – or give up, since joke telling is a skill best left to pros.

"What was his/is your name again?"
→ Use the name/face memory techniques outlined in the previous section, as recalling names/faces are their own different system.

"The name is familiar but I can't seem to remember what he looks like/put a face to the name"
→ Use the name/face memory techniques outlined in the previous section, as recalling names/faces are their own different system.

KEY REVIEW POINTS

Memory glitches can begin happening in our early 20s – the forgetting of someone familiar's name, the on-the-tip-of-my-tongue word that remains stubborn out of reach. While these glitches become more frequent with age, they are in no way a precursor of pending dementia or a warning sign of Alzheimer's certainty. Embarrassing, but no cause for real concern, and is 'treatable'!

The main issue with memory is that the encoding system used to put an item into long term storage was either faulty or unknown, nonexistent – no system used – so retrieval is also faulty or nonexistent.

The only way to retrieve past memories that were encoded wrong and have no direct current connection to them is to recreate the environment as much as possible when the memory occurred – go to the place, see the same sights, smell the same smells, hear the same sounds – locking in as many of the memory elements as possible often allows the memories to come flooding back.

This can be done on site, but locations change over time as little stays the same, and it's impossible to physically go back and recreate the past 100%. But the mind is very powerful and can recreate the past, if you sit quietly and allow your imagination free reign.

[**The reason it's hard to recapture** all the learning that we gained at school is because the unique learning environment experienced at that youthful time is impossible to reproduce; all the people who were a part of the school experience are no longer young!]

The key to improving memory is to have a system and use it moving forward to encode new memories. Choose whatever link-peg is most comfortable to you, that you will use regularly and habitually. Adopting a system, making it yours, as a part of your daily routine is the path to encoding retrievable memories.

Writing it down helps a lot – even if you never look back on your notes – because you are touching it with multiple senses: physical touch (of the pen in your hand) and vision (seeing the written words as you write them). This is why To-Do list are commonly jotted down; if you forgot where you put the list, you can sometimes see the list in your mind's eye.

Students take notes in class to study from, but the actual writing of the notes is a big part of the recall process.

The main memory solutions – CRITICAL:
use right away, lock in the memory as it occurs

Absentmindedness → use ASSOCIATON

Short-term memory retrieval
→ 1) use VISUAL AIDS, help support memory
with any visual means possible, since relying
on your brain to simply remember without a
connection is not how the brain works!

→ 2) use ROTE, repeating over and over does
hold in short term memory for a short time,
but is limited in how many items can be held at
once, usually 4-7 is capacity, with diminishing
accuracy.

Long-term memory retrieval
→ use a LINK-PEG system. Link the item to an
established peg, use the same system over
and over again for great recall. The key is to
create really vivid images, with as many wild
memory elements as possible!!

The SmartyPants Secret
on MEMORY

If it's not moving, the brain is prone to not 'see' it, so the mind needs to create movement to recall things.

We are programmed to see what moves – a possible dangerous threat – and we tend to miss what doesn't move. Allow the brain to see the memory by giving it the movement right in the moment that the needs for best recall; create movement by constructing an outlandish moving mental image, using multiple senses and elements. Once seen, the brain will then remember!

Having a memory system and knowing how to use it are important factors, but the *critical* secret is to actually use the system; to take a split second and create the mental visual association right in the moment immediately after it happens. This allows the brain to do what it does best, allowing anyone at any age to have a good retrievable memory – yes, including YOU!

BOOK BONUS

As a thank you to buyers, there is an additional free resource available only to book buyers. Did you get yours? If you missed it, go to www.SmartyPantsSecrets.com/bookbonus .

It has additional valuable content and is free to book buyers, so don't miss out on getting yours!

BOOK RESOURCE

This SmartyPants Secrets book has a companion resource on the topic that may be of interest. The resource for this Memory Book is a **100% natural organic _Herbal Blend Memory Aid_, to support memory retention.**

This **_Herbal Blend Memory Aid_** not only works to support memory function, it also tastes great, and makes a lovely gift for others you care about that may be experiencing memory impairment issues.

For ordering and other information on this and other SmartyPants Secrets support products, visit the website at www.SmartyPantsSecrets.com/resources

ABOUT ME

I am DR Martin, PhD* (*Personal human Development expertise) – Dolley Rapoport Martin. I took Dolley as my first name* in honor of the great First Lady Dolley Madison, whom I admire for her heroic actions in the White House during very turbulent times.

I took Rapoport as a middle name* in honor of Ingeborg Rapoport, who at age 103, is the oldest person to be awarded a Doctorate; finally getting the recognition due her from 77 years prior in Nazi Germany, unfairly denied her due to her Jewish roots. There is so much injustice in the world; it is an honor to recognize her achievement by taking her name.   [*The selecting of one's name is an important exercise, since names are so personal and tied to identity. Yet most of us go through life with a name not of our choosing. Check out the SmartyPants Secret book NAMES.]

I have studied every communication subject for more than a decade, acquiring a large body of knowledge. I, perhaps like you, am a voracious reader and learner. My other strength is that I retain much of what I learn, so I can then compile the knowledge on a variety of subjects into a concise format, making the books that I author a shortcut on the best knowledge available. This saves you from going through all the data looking for the kernel that makes the greatest difference in success, the SmartyPants Secret on a given topic.

I also have a mind that is ever curious about so many topics. I have earned multiple expert designations (education certified English teacher, Real Estate Broker, Stock Broker series 7, series 6, Certified Financial Manager, Insurance producer certified, Coach University) and held high level and leadership positions in business – large corporate entities, privately held companies, non-profit organizations, and startups – plus have volunteered extensively, holding executive positions at the local, district and national levels. So I've been around the block more than once, on more than one topic.

Due to my research and experience, I have logged the perquisite time to carry the title of expert, giving myself an honorary PhD* in the expertise area of communication, *Personal human Development. I am passionate about sharing the knowledge that I have gained with you, in bite-size pieces.

And when a certain topic is not in my field of expertise, I find an expert with deep expertise in the field who has the knowledge that I seek, pass it on, in a book on the subject.

SMARTYp∙nts
secrets

For other titles and additional resources, visit
www.SmartyPantsSecrets.com

Watch for content clips and helpful technique
tips on a variety of topics coming soon at
www.youtube.com/c/smartypantssecrets

Contact: Info@SmartyPantsSecrets.com